Kids love reading
Choose Your O...

"I loved the twis...
the different ...gs."
Karianne Morehouse, age 12

"This is a flashlight-under-your-covers-book
to read at night. It's exciting, thrilling
and fun all at the same time."
Walker Curtis, age 11

"I like the places the author chose to put the
choices. It really makes it hard to put down
the book because it's like you're in the story."
Haley Behn, age 11

"It's really cool how you get to choose the end!
It made the book really fun to read."
Josh Farber, age 12

THE ABOMINABLE SNOWMAN

BY R. A. MONTGOMERY

ILLUSTRATED BY LAURENCE PEGUY
COVER ILLUSTRATED BY JOSE LUIS MARRON

sundance™

Illustrated by: Laurence Peguy
Cover illustrated by: Jose Luis Marron
Book design: Stacey Hood, Big Eyedea Visual Design

For information regarding permission, write to:

A Haights Cross Communications Company

Sundance Publishing
P.O. Box 740
One Beeman Road
Northborough, MA 01532-0740
800-343-8204
www.sundancepub.com

ISBN 0-7608-9693-3

Published simultaneously in the United States and Canada

This book is dedicated to

Anson and Ramsey

and to Roland Palmedo

BEWARE and WARNING!

This book is different from other books.

You and YOU ALONE are in charge of what happens in this story.

There are dangers, choices, adventures and consequences. YOU must use all of your numerous talents and much of your enormous intelligence. The wrong decision could end in disaster—even death. But, don't despair. At anytime, YOU can go back and make another choice, alter the path of your story, and change its result.

You and your best friend Carlos have traveled to Nepal in search of the fabled *Yeti* or abominable snowman. Last year while the two of you were mountain climbing in South America, a guide told you about the legendary creature and you haven't stopped thinking about the *Yeti* since. Carlos arrived and went straight into the mountains when a *Yeti* sighting was reported. He hasn't been heard from in three days. A late monsoon storm has moved in and the mountains are almost impassable. You know Carlos will depend on you to do the right thing. But what is it?

You are a mountain climber. Three years ago you spent the summer at a climbing school in the mountains of Colorado. Your instructors said that you had natural skills as a climber. You made rapid progress, and by the end of the summer you were leading difficult rock and ice climbs.

That summer, you became close friends with a boy named Carlos. The two of you made a good climbing team. Last year you and he were chosen to join an international team. The expedition made it to the top of two unclimbed peaks in South America.

One night on that expedition, the group was seated around the cook tent at the base camp. The expedition leader, Franz, told stories of climbing in the Himalayas, the highest mountains in the world.

Turn to page 2, then to page 4.

THE HIMALAYA MOUNTAINS

Annapùrnà

Machapùchàre

Lhots

Gosàìnthan

Changtse

Katmandu

The Himalayas form a great natural wall between India and China, with Nepal tucked in amid the peaks. Everest, K2, and Annapurna are the best-known mountains in the Himalayas. These and many other peaks have been climbed. Still others lie in remote areas where few humans have gone. There, said Franz, in the high valleys beneath the snowfields, lives the *Yeti*, sometimes called the Abominable Snowman.

"The *Yeti* is said to be a huge beast," Franz tells you, "perhaps a cross between a gorilla and a human. People cannot agree what it is."

"Is the *Yeti* dangerous?" Carlos asked.

Franz shrugged. "Some say it is. Other people say the *Yeti* is very gentle."

"Have you ever seen one?" you inquire.

"No. Almost no one has. The best proof of the *Yeti*'s existence is a set of very large footprints discovered in the 1950s by a British expedition. No one has ever photographed one that I have heard," Franz answers. "But still the stories persist."

Go on to the next page.

You and Carlos decided then and there to find the *Yeti*. When you returned from South America, the two of you raised money from the International Foundation For Research Into Strange Phenomena. Your goal: proof positive that *Yeti* exist. You will find and photograph the *Yeti*.

That is what brings you to Kathmandu, the capital of Nepal. Your problems, though, have already begun. Two days ago Carlos left by helicopter to look over the terrain near Mt. Everest. The helicopter returned without him. The pilot told you that Carlos decided to stay up at the Everest base camp to check out a report that a *Yeti* had been seen. He had a radio transmitter, but you have received no word from him. The weather turned bad and radio communication was interrupted.

You have an appointment to speak with R. N. Runal, the Director of Expeditions and Mountain Research and an authority on the *Yeti*. He knows of your plans. You need his help with official permits for the expedition. He will also have good advice and information.

But what about Carlos?

If you decide to cancel your meeting with Runal and search for Carlos, turn to page 7.

If you feel that Carlos is OK and go ahead with your plan to meet Runal, turn to page 8.

You telephone Mr. Runal at the Foreign Ministry. "This is an emergency, Mr. Runal. My friend Carlos is missing at base camp. I need help, right now!"

"Of course. I understand. Please allow me the honor of coming with you. I know the region well."

You gladly accept the help of Mr. Runal. His reputation as a mountaineer is excellent. He is able to arrange for a Royal Nepalese Army helicopter to meet you at the Tribuhavan Airport.

Two hours later you land at the Everest base camp where Carlos was last seen. His red nylon mountain tent is still there, but the storm has erased all footprints.

"Most reports of the *Yeti* have them well below base camp. But it is possible that they are up this high," Runal says as the two of you stand by the tent looking at the glacier and the high peaks.

If you and Runal search below the base camp in the valley, turn to page 9.

If you go above the base camp, turn to page 13.

You walk down a street bordered by tall pines. They are green-blue, and the branches and needles are very fine and delicate. Hanging from the upper branches are what look like huge, tear shaped, blackish-brown fruit. You stop and look up, wondering what they are. Then one moves, spreads giant wings, and flaps off. They are bats, the largest bats you have ever seen!

You reach the Foreign Ministry, and you are shown to a waiting room. You wait a few minutes and then are ushered in to meet R. N. Runal, Director of Expeditions and Mountain Research for the Nepalese government.

"Welcome to our country. We wish you success. But I have some bad news. The expedition you have proposed could be very dangerous."

You look at him, not knowing what to expect.

Turn to page 10.

The helicopter stays at base camp, and you and Runal descend on foot along a narrow, rocky path below the snow line into a pine forest. It takes many hours of careful walking.

The trail suddenly becomes very steep, and one side falls off more than a thousand meters to a river gorge. You come to a small stone house with a thatched roof. An old woman sits in the sunlight by the door.

"Can you tell us if any climbers came by here? My friend is about five foot nine, medium build, has dark hair." Runal translates your description into Nepali.

The woman nods and says two men came by. The younger one left a note:

Runal turns to you with a puzzled look on his face.

"Carlos is your friend. If it were up to me, I would ignore his message. But you know him better. What now? What do you think?"

If you obey the message and climb back up to the base camp to wait for Carlos, turn to page 20.

If you ignore the message and decide to look for Carlos, turn to page 15.

10

"Recently, a large expedition set out without telling us that they were going after the *Yeti*," says Runal. "They used guns and traps, and tried to kill one of them. The *Yeti* are angry."

"Mr. Runal, we just want to find a *Yeti*. We have no intention of ever hurting a *Yeti*."

"I know that. We have checked up on you. It is a shame about the others. I must advise against going into *Yeti* territory—I could arrange a trip for you into the Terai region, out of the mountains, in the jungle area. You could photograph and study the tigers. They are famous, and also dangerous. Later, perhaps, you could conduct the expedition you are leading."

If you decide to go ahead with the expedition for the Yeti, turn to page 16.

If you decide to postpone the expedition to let the Yeti calm down and go on to the Terai region in search of tigers, turn to page 19.

Above the base camp are the dangerous "seracs." These huge blocks of ice are always moving, and people climbing through this maze of ice are in constant danger. Runal leads the way. You both have crampons on your boots. A slender red and yellow nylon rope links the two of you. It's a safety rope. "Watch out! Jump!"

A block of ice quivers and tumbles to the side, sending clouds of snow and ice crystals in the air. Runal had seen it just in time. You move more slowly now, wary of these treacherous seracs.

On the back side of a serac as large as a two-story house, you find him. Carlos is sitting in the sun, fidgeting with his camera.

"Hey, what are you guys doing here?"

"That's what we want to know. You scared us to death with your disappearing act. What's up?"

Carlos puts the camera away and, after you introduce him to Runal, explains that he found tracks, *Yeti* tracks perhaps, and followed them. He tried to radio, but the weather blocked it. The tracks faded, and he couldn't find his way back to the camp. He had been sitting and waiting. Runal examines one track protected from drifting snow, and explains that they are blue bear tracks and not *Yeti* tracks.

So, disappointed, you go back to the helicopter and return to Kathmandu.

Turn to page 14.

14

The next day you go to the shop of Sangee Podang Sorba, a well-known Sherpa guide. Carlos stays with Runal, getting the permits.

You enter the store and there, behind a counter stacked with dried food in plastic bags, tanks of gas for mountain stoves, and wool hats, is Sangee Sorba. You introduce yourself, and immediately you like this man. He is warm and friendly, and recently he has been with the Japanese expedition to Pumori and a French Everest attempt.

Maybe you should ask him to join you as you search for the *Yeti*.

If you ask Sangee to come along in your expedition, turn to page 23.

If you wait and decide to talk it over with Carlos, turn to page 22.

"Carlos may be in trouble. We must find him."

Runal nods in agreement, and he gives the woman two copper coins. She smiles at him and speaks rapidly in Nepali. Then she shuffles into the house. You and Runal remain outside, next to the small garden where squash lie ripening.

"What was that all about? What did the old woman say?" You adjust your rucksack straps to stop them from chafing your shoulders.

Runal looks at you and says, "The woman claims that your friend was traveling with a *Yeti*."

You stare at Runal in disbelief But why not? You are here to find them; maybe they found you this time.

You head down the trail not knowing quite what to expect.

Turn to page 32.

"I appreciate your warning and kind offer of the alternative to go to the Terai," you say. "We are committed to this expedition. We will search for the *Yeti* with openness and friendship."

R. N. Runal nods his head and speaks quickly to his assistant in Nepali. Within minutes you have the necessary papers for the expedition, stamped in the proper places with the official seal of the Nepalese government. As you shake hands before leaving, he stops you. "If you are determined to go on your expedition, it could be easier and safer if I come with you."

What should you do? Having a government official along with you might just cause delays and bureaucratic snafus. On the other hand, he could also smooth the way.

*If you accept Runal's offer to join you,
turn to page 24.*

If you decline his offer, turn to page 27.

You talk with Runal at length about the Terai, a tropical zone at sea level just one hundred miles from Everest, the highest elevation on earth. What contrast! You realize that it will make excellent material for a feature article for your local paper.

"The Terai is incredible," Runal tells you. "The jungle is filled with flowers and animals, the fierce Indian tiger, and the dangerous rhinoceros. I will arrange to have elephants carry you into the remote areas."

Within two days, after leaving a message for Carlos, you are riding on an elephant's back, swaying with its ponderous footsteps.

The heat is almost unbearable, and drops of sweat roll down your neck and soak your khaki safari shirt.

You come to a stream bordered by thick green jungle. There, in the sand, are boot prints and spent cartridges from a large weapon.

"Not good. Not good. Must be poachers after tiger skins and elephant tusks. Dangerous," says your guide.

"Let's follow them. Let's see what they're up to."

"OK, but maybe we should split up; that way we can cover more territory."

If you split up, turn to page 28.

If you stay together, turn to page 29.

"Probably best to return to base camp," you say. However, it is getting late, and the trail back up will be especially dangerous at night.

"I think we should stay here until dawn," Runal counters.

You make arrangements with the woman to spend the night. She brings a simple meal of rice, squash, and buttered tea. You are very nervous, but you trust Carlos's judgment. Whatever is going on is out of your hands for now, anyway.

You can't sleep, and the wind of the high mountains keeps you restless and heightens your worry.

Close to dawn, you hear a high, piercing scream.

Turn to page 31.

You're quick, but not quick enough. Sangee drops the axe and pulls both your arms behind your back.

The two men who were in the doorway are now inside the store. One of them shuts the door and bolts it. The click of the bolt, locking you in and help out, is ominous.

The three men surround you.

"Foolish one. Now you have gone too far. Why are you here? What do you want?" Sangee snarls at you.

The man with the beard holds a small, ugly looking automatic pistol.

"I meant no harm. I just wanted to see what was inside the pocket."

"Well, there's no way out. We need both of you for our plan. You will send a message to your friend, telling him you've found an important clue. Get him to come here. If you don't, we'll kill you on the spot. If you do as we say, well, maybe you'll live. We'll have to see. We've been following you two. We thought we would use you to get this stuff out of the country."

He points at packages wrapped in brown paper. What's in it, you wonder? This is an awful position to be in. What do you do now?

If you say you'll write the note to Carlos, turn to page 46.

If you refuse, turn to page 47.

You think Carlos should have a chance to meet Sangee. You occupy yourself with buying the high altitude tents, ice axes, crampons, ropes, pitons, and ice screws.

While looking through a rack of down-filled parkas used on previous mountain expeditions, you come across one that attracts your attention. It's a purple parka, medium-sized. One of the pockets is filled with something.

You give a quick look around the shop to make sure that no one is watching and undo the velcro flap. It feels like there's a rock in the pocket. You take it out and unwrap the heavy brown paper that covers it. It's a skull!!! Could this be a *Yeti* skull? Yikes! There is a piece of paper stuffed inside the skull.

It's a map, and it shows a road leading from Kathmandu to the town of Nagarkot. There is an X marked next to an abandoned temple of the Hindu god Shiva.

Turn to page 34.

"How about joining us on our search for the *Yeti*, Sangee?"

He smiles and hesitates. Then he picks up two sticks of incense. One is longer than the other. He lights them both, and their rich fragrance fills the air of his small store.

"You see, as one fragrance merges with the other we do not know the difference between them. Only when the shorter stick burns out will we know which stick was the fragrance of rose and which was the fragrance of magnolia."

You are puzzled by his talk of incense. You ask, "So, what does that mean, Sangee?"

"It does not mean anything, it only IS."

You are really confused now. What to do? Perhaps you should leave this talk of incense alone and forget about asking Sangee to join you. Maybe he's crazy.

If you back out of the offer to take him on the expedition, turn to page 33.

If you persist and try to understand his point, turn to page 38.

24

Now that he's a member of your expedition, Runal sends out a government team to set up your base camp and find Carlos. Success! Carlos is found and rejoins you. Runal turns out to be an excellent team member. Six porters carry your food and tents and supplies. This leaves you free to explore the steep valley sides and the small villages along the way.

The days are long, beginning at first light and going until sunset. Your legs ache from the constant pounding as you walk along the narrow trails which have served these Nepalese people for hundreds of years. Above you are bright blue skies dotted with clouds. The snow and ice flanks of Lhotse, Pumori, and Everest rise above the green of the lower slopes.

Turn to page 26.

As you approach a village, Runal points out a large building with a red roof, which stands above the small, neat houses clustered about it.

"That's the monastery where there lives a monk, a Buddhist monk, who has lived with the *Yeti*."

"But I thought no one had really seen one. I thought no one alive had spent time with the *Yeti*."

Runal answers, "A well-kept secret. Those who share the secret knowledge of the *Yeti* are pledged to reveal this knowledge only to appointed people. You, and you alone, are one of the appointed. It has been seen in the stars; it has been read in your hand."

"What do you mean? Who saw it in the stars? Who read it in my hand?"

Runal does not answer for several minutes. Then he speaks. "If you accept the secret knowledge, your life will change. You will never be the same. Decide now."

If you are ready for the secret knowledge of the Yeti, and the responsibility that goes with it, turn to page 40.

If you reject the offer of secret knowledge, turn to page 116.

"I think we'll go it alone, thanks, anyway." Mr. Runal shakes your hand, but he does not smile. It is clear that you have offended this man.

What should you do? Is an apology in order? Should you try to patch things up?

If you try to make amends and end up inviting him to accompany you, turn to page 39.

If you stick to your decision, turn to page 42.

28

"OK," you say to the guide, "you go on down-stream. I'll head into the jungle and circle around and meet you at the stream. If you need help, fire three shots, wait six seconds, and fire three more shots."

"OK. Be careful."

You set off into the jungle, moving as quietly as possible. Two hours later you stop for a rest, swatting at the mosquitoes and picking off the leeches. With a roar, a magnificent tiger, at least eight feet in length from nose to tail, springs out of the brush.

You are finished.

The End

You and your guide head downstream. You find the poachers. Killing tigers and elephants for their skins and tusks is a serious crime in Nepal. They don't believe in leaving evidence of their activities. You try running away into the forest, but the poachers are quick. They don't leave any witnesses.

The End

"Yeeeeeowee!!!"

The noise seems to be coming from right outside your window. Runal moves quickly to the doorway. The woman is outside the house at the edge of the trail, holding up a battered kerosene lantern.

You hear the cry again. This time it is even louder.

"Yeoweee!! Yi, Yi, Yeeeoweee!!"

Suddenly the sound diminishes. It seems to be going farther and farther away. The woman waves her lantern. Is it a signal, or is she trying to frighten whatever it was away?

"Those are the *Yeti*," she says. "They invite you to join them and your friend Carlos."

What should you do? This is more than you had bargained for.

You look at Runal, and then at the woman. It is chilly in the half-light of morning. The *Yeti* sound is growing fainter by the minute.

If you follow the sound of the Yeti,
turn to page 43.

If you return to the base camp and
the helicopter, turn to page 45.

As you race down the path you see footprints that might have been left by a Yeti. Suddenly it is very quiet. The birds have stopped singing. The only sound you hear is your footsteps and Runal's right behind you. You wonder why.

It doesn't take long to find out. Around a turn in the path you run smack into a band of creatures that can only be Yeti. They are aiming an ancient bronze cannon at you. One of them touches a light to the fuse.

And that is the last thing you remember—until you wake up in your own bed. It must have been the awesome tripledecker with mustard, anchovies, and chocolate syrup.

The End

"I don't think I understand. Before you come with us, I'd better talk with my partner. He's not far away. I'll go find him now. If I don't come back, don't wait for me."

You move slowly toward the door; the incense smoke gets dense. In an instant it is so thick that you can't find the door. Gradually you lose consciousness and drift into a lifelong coma.

The End

34

This is too exciting to wait for Carlos. *Carpe Diem,* as they say. You walk over to the counter and ask Sangee where the parka came from.

Sangee looks up in surprise. There is fear in his eyes when he sees you holding up the purple parka.

"Oh, that is not for sale. That is a mistake to have it here. Please give it to me. Give it to me!!"

You look in the parka and there, near the collar, is Sangee's name stenciled in black ink. You look up and see Sangee moving toward you with an ice axe in his hand. He raises the ice axe. You throw the parka at him. It's enough to startle him. You run for the door, but standing there are two tough-looking men. One has a beard, and the other is clean-shaven with hair hanging down to his shoulders. You jive to the right, duck to the left, and make for the rack of ice axes at the back of the shop.

Turn to page 21.

Run! You run for your life! You dash for the trees at the edge of the cliff. Maybe you can hide there. The *Yeti* is fast, faster than you ever thought.

Then you are falling, slipping into space over the cliff. Miraculously, the *Yeti* reaches out and grabs you, saving you just in time from certain death. He carries you back to your tent, puts you down gently, and slips off into the night.

The End

38

"OK, so you want me to choose which stick is rose and which is magnolia. Is that it? Is it a test? If I'm right you'll go, if not you won't?"

Sangee smiles, displaying gold caps on three of his upper front teeth. He nods his head.

"Here goes," you say. "The longer stick is Kashmiri Rose incense."

Sangee claps his hands, brings them up to his forehead, and bows slightly, saying, "Namaste, bara sahib. I am at your command, Master."

It is decided. He will accompany you. You have chosen the right one.

Some things just happen by chance. This was one of them. You ask, "Where should we head? Annapurna or the Lhotse-Everest region? What do you think, Sangee?"

"Many have seen *Yeti* prints near Everest, but there is the region near Annapurna and Machapuchhre (Fish Tail Mountain) where we could have good luck. The Everest region has been more fully explored; Annapurna is less well known."

If you choose the Annapurna region,
turn to page 50.

If you choose the Everest region,
turn to page 48.

"Mr. Runal, I beg your pardon, sir. I have made a mistake. This is your country, and we need your help. Please do accompany us. It will be our honor and pleasure to have you with us."

The room is silent. You shift nervously and stare out the window at the palace grounds and the formal gardens.

Runal does not respond right away. He fiddles with a pencil on his desk, deep in thought.

"I appreciate the kind offer. I can only accept if you allow me the great honor of being expedition leader. If you will allow this, I may be able to arrange for funds from the government, as well as tactical support from the Royal Nepalese Army, including helicopters."

This catches you by surprise. You are the leader.

If you allow him to be expedition leader,
turn to page 52.

If you point out that it will not be possible,
turn to page 54.

"I gladly accept your offer. I am ready for the knowledge."

"Come with me." He leads you to the monastery. Carlos stays behind.

You and Runal enter the monastery through a huge wooden door. It is dark inside, but you make out the figure of an old man seated on the floor. Behind him is a statue of Buddha. The man welcomes you and motions you to sit before him. You see that he is wearing the robes of a monk. You are served yak-butter tea, a thick broth that you find hard to swallow.

"Listen well with heart, head, and body. Listen with eyes more than with ears. Heed the cry of the Yeti," the old monk tells you.

You can hear bells in the distance and wind in the pine trees just outside the window. It is beautiful.

You sit for what seems like hours, listening with your whole being.

Finally, the monk speaks.

"Time now to go on the next journey."

"What journey?" you ask. This is getting too weird.

"A continuation of the one you are already on," he replies.

If you agree to take the journey, turn to page 51.

If you decide that you are not prepared to change your life forever, turn to page 63.

You leave Runal's office. As you walk outside you are hit with torrential rain. It falls from the sky, hitting the earth in explosive drops. You planned your expedition assuming the monsoons would be over by now, but apparently they are not.

You sit it out in your hotel for three weeks. The constant rain has closed off the trails to the mountain valleys with mudslides and boulders. Nature has gone wild and your expedition is blocked for good. Too bad. Try again next season.

The End

You run down the trail with Runal following.

Minutes later you jerk to a halt. There in front of you is the body of a yak, the ox of the high mountains. Its horns have been savagely twisted off. They are now used as markers to point the way from the path to a thick rhododendron-and-pine grove.

You pause, looking at the horrible sight of the dead yak. The horns may be pointing you to Carlos, or they may lead into a trap.

If you take Runal with you into the grove for added protection, turn to page 58.

If you leave Runal behind as a rear guard, because one person can move more quietly and quickly, and go into the grove by yourself, turn to page 62.

"We've got to get back up to the base camp," you say.

Runal grabs your arm." I know that cry. It's the battle cry, the cry of anger and revenge. We'll get help and come back for Carlos."

"Why are they angry? We have done nothing to them."

"Too many people have hunted them, tormented them. They have had enough," Runal answers.

The trail seems much steeper. Finally you are at the edge of the glacier where the camp was pitched. The light of the late morning sun nearly blinds you as it flashes off the ice.

The helicopter lies smashed in the snow. The rotor blades are twisted and the Plexiglas is shattered. There is no sign of the pilot, just giant footprints—*Yeti* footprints—leading off to the heart of the icefall.

If you follow the prints, turn to page 57.

*If you stay by the shattered helicopter,
hoping for help, turn to page 55.*

"I'll get Carlos here. I'm not sure where he is, though," you say.

The muzzle of the automatic wavers, points at you, and then the man holding the gun lowers it and slips it into his pocket. For the time being it looks as though the danger is over.

How can you get out of luring Carlos into this trap? You remember a special signal used when climbing with ropes. Three sharp tugs on the rope meant trouble.

"Okay, give me pen and paper." They hand you these things and you begin to write.

"Hey, this pen doesn't work. Look!"

You quickly scratch three lines on the paper with the pen. Of course it works, and you say, "Well, I guess it's working now."

You hope that the three marks are enough to warn Carlos. You need time to plan your escape.

The bearded man speaks in a German accent.

"Tell us now what you know about the map."

If you make up a fantastic story,
turn to page 59.

If you insist that you know nothing,
turn to page 64.

"Never, never. I'm not falling for your stuff. If you want Carlos, then go after him yourself."

At that very moment there is a loud knock on the door.

"Open up. Police. You're surrounded." The door crashes open and three Nepalese soldiers and a police officer rush in. Carlos is behind them.

The officer nods at the strangers and says, "Hands up. Well, well, we finally got you, didn't we? It's jail for you. Smugglers are all the same. Fortunately, we have been following you for the last three weeks. When you started following these two, we followed them also. Carlos has helped us. Your smuggling days are over."

You are badly shaken, but the Nepalese government now considers you and Carlos heroes, and they will give you all the help you need for your expedition.

The End

48

You had always wanted to explore the Everest region first. It is the area where the villages are, and the Sherpas are the most famous mountain climbers and guides on the expeditions in these giant Himalayan mountains. Sangee comes from a village in the Everest region, and that alone could be most helpful in getting porters and help if needed.

Later that week you, Carlos, and Sangee board a single-engine aircraft and fly for more than two hours deep into the Himalayas, skirting Pumori

and Lhotse, and banking gracefully around Everest.

The air strip is short and very bumpy. You marvel at the skill with which the Royal Nepal Airlines pilot sets the plane down ever so gently.

The air is thin at this altitude of four thousand meters, but it is clear. The mountains, with their snowfields and serpentine glaciers, glisten and sparkle. You feel dizzy both from the height and the beauty of the scene.

Turn to page 68.

50

Two days later, with permits obtained and supplies bought, you, Carlos, and Sangee start the long journey from Kathmandu to Pokhara.

Three days after that, you and your party, along with twelve porters to carry the supplies, are camped in a field high above the valley floor near a small village called Dhumpus.

That night, after a dinner of brown rice and lentils, onions, and garlic, you sit in front of your red mountain tents watching the moon play on the snowy white flanks of Annapurna and Dhaulagiri. It is silent and chilly. You are tired from the climb, but glad to be alive and in this magical kingdom. With the darkened village behind you, you feel as though your group might be the only people on Earth.

Surprisingly you see a light flash on Annapurna. It repeats. Then again. It may just be a reflection, or another party, or it may be a signal from someone in trouble. Or maybe it's a signal from from the *Yeti*.

If you think it is a signal, turn to page 67.

If you think it is just another climbing party, turn to page 65.

Runal is still with you. He taps you on the shoulder, and you rise and follow him to the back of the monastery behind the golden Buddha. The heavy smell of rose-scented incense fills the air.

"The *Yeti* are guides to Shangri-La. They take the chosen people to this hidden valley, which many have heard of and only a few have seen."

You nod, wondering what comes next.

"One last chance, my friend. Turn back now and live a normal life with your friend Carlos. Go ahead and accept the life of the secret world."

If you go on, turn to page 70.

If you turn back, turn to page 72.

52

"OK, Mr. Runal, you lead the expedition; I'm sure our goals are the same. We can use the support of your government." Runal's connections within the government turn out to be very useful. Soon the expedition has better supplies and equipment than you would have been able to get on your own. His knowledge about the *Yeti* proves to be useful. Arrangements for a helicopter to the base camp at Mt. Everest are made. Maybe it's the best to have him lead. It's his land, and he knows it well.

Turn to page 24.

54

The telephone rings, breaking the silence in the room. Runal excuses himself and picks it up.

"Yes. Yes. I understand… I will tell them."

He turns to you with a serious look on his face. "Our king is upset that people are disturbing the peace of our land. He apologizes, but he has decided to close the mountains to all expeditions. It is time for a rest. The *Yeti* are not animals. We will not allow them to be hunted any more. I am sorry, my friend."

Well, at least you didn't have to refuse Runal's offer of leadership.

The End

You stay near the remains of the camp, following Carlos's instructions. Runal agrees that this is the right thing to do.

"You see, my friend, the high mountains, this roof of the world, they hold secrets, mysteries, dangers. We have trespassed. We should wait and see what happens."

You wait for a while, but you decide that you have to do something to save Carlos. Maybe the old woman lied. Maybe she made up the story about Carlos being with the *Yeti*. Maybe the weird cries were some kind of temple horn down in the valley. Maybe it was phony. But why? You are confused.

"Runal, I'm going back down after Carlos. You stay here if you wish. I can't leave him."

Runal agrees, but he stays to wait for a search helicopter.

Turn to page 76.

The prints lead you into the intricate maze in the icefall. You must be careful, because even the slightest movement of the glacier could cause ice seracs to collapse. This is a death zone! Then, abruptly, the footprints stop. They just stop, as if the owners of the feet suddenly sprouted wings and flew away.

You look all around at the shimmering ice, at the compacted snow, at the sharp gray and brown of rock flanked by ice. Overhead, several enormous birds soar in the thermals. On the summit of the mountains, curls of snow looking like smoke rise in the gathering wind.

You and Runal stand in awe of the mountains, momentarily forgetting your mission.

Something catches your eye. It's a piece of red nylon cloth held down by a small chunk of ice. Could it be from Carlos's tent? You investigate and, as you stoop to pick it up, you hear a sudden noise.

Turn to page 75.

58

Cautiously, you and Runal enter the grove. The pale light of dawn does little to illuminate this eerie place. You are both careful not to make noise.

Runal tugs at your sleeve and points to the branches of a pine. Hanging from the branches is a red backpack. You approach cautiously. It looks like the pack that Carlos had been carrying. It may have been taken from him, or he might have left it as a warning.

If you retreat now and go for more help, turn to page 77.

If you give the special bird call whistle that you and Carlos use as your emergency code, turn to page 80.

"Well, you see, it's like this. I am the prince of a tribe of superior beings from the lost continent of Atlantis. We live under the sea off the coast of Africa. Now we are ready to join forces with the *Yeti*, a tribe from the planet Borodoz which has been in the high mountains for the last three hundred years."

The three look at you and begin to laugh. One of them says, "Sure, and I'm Julius Caesar, and here is Cleopatra." They all laugh at the big joke. This gives you time to whip out your Swiss Army knife. You cut some cords hanging from the ceiling. A mountain tent on display falls down on top of your enemies. You scoot out the door just in time.

You forget about supplies for now, and go to the police. Later you decide to cancel the expedition for this season. There will always be another chance.

The End

60

Carlos is in the center of a group of people. While you look on in amazement, some of the people change form before your very eyes. One moment they are *Yeti*, and the next, unicorns. Smiling, Carlos speaks to you.

"Welcome. You have completed a difficult journey and found your way to knowledge. Now begins the true journey."

The End

You ask yourself why you are doing this. Who knows what's in there? But Carlos is in danger, so you enter the thicket. The pale light barely penetrates the pine trees. After fifteen minutes of slow progress, you come across a strange-looking fence. It seems to be made of some kind of aluminum or stainless steel.

You test it, and a gate swings open. Peculiar that it was not locked. A well-worn path leads to a rock face. At the base of the rock face, there is a strange carving.

A bright red door leads into the rock wall, and a path leads away from the wall. What now?

If you enter the door, turn to page 82.

If you follow the path, turn to page 81.

You get up and head for the door. An invisible barrier stops you. The monk smiles. Perhaps he understands your feelings of conflict.

"I'm not too happy being here. I'm frightened."

The monk says, "Nothing is easy; many things are frightening. If you must leave, then leave. You will return when you are ready."

You thank the monk. This time nothing blocks you from going through the door. Several minutes later you look back, not knowing whether you made the right choice or not. Your memory of the recent past events is blurring, slipping, vanishing.

The End

64

"I know nothing, nothing."

The bearded one scowls and says, "That's what they all say. Let's end it right here. That expedition for the *Yeti* is phony. They're all from Interpol."

"Hey, I'll make a deal." You don't have the faintest idea what kind of a "deal" you could offer, but you need to stall for time. Then, to your immense surprise, Sangee opens the back door, and six men holding weapons enter.

"Gentlemen, you are under arrest." He flashes a badge and smiles at you. "Sorry, my friend. You just came here at the wrong time. I had to attack you to keep these men from becoming suspicious. The map you found will lead us to their hidden supplies. Good luck on your expedition.

The End

"Let's watch it. I'm not sure that it's anything more than someone playing with a flashlight."

For the next two hours you sit and watch the spot where the flashes came from. But the flashing has stopped. It's cold now, and you are glad to have your parkas. The stars are bright, and you are awed by the immensity of the mountains before you. No wonder so many people have been attracted to them.

You turn in, tired from the long hike and anxious to get on with the search for the *Yeti*.

Four hours later, at about 2 A.M., you are awakened by a wailing noise near your tent.

Yeeeeeeeeee Ah, Ah, Ah!!

Yeeeeeeeeee Ah, Ah, Ah!!!!

You unzip the tent flap and peer out into the darkness.

There, near the pile of gear, is a dark mass. Maybe it's a *Yeti*. You reach for your camera. Maybe you can get a picture.

Then the mass rears up and lurches for the tents where Carlos and Sangee are sleeping.

What should you do? If you want to click the picture, turn to page 86.

If you decide instead to grab an ice axe and try to frighten this creature, turn to page 87.

"Look at at that flashing light, Carlos!" Once again the light blinks three times, then stops. Then it blinks again. "What do you think? Could be trouble."

Sangee says, "That could be an emergency signal. But it is very far from here, across the valley and just below the glacier. We could go, or I could return to Pokhara and report it to the authorities."

"How much time would it take you to get back to Pokhara?"

"I can go faster than our whole group. Perhaps it would take a day, and they would send a helicopter. Without outside help, there is little we could do if there is someone in trouble. But they may need help quickly."

Should you respond to the call for help?
If so, turn to page 85.

If you decide to let Sangee return to
Pokhara for help, turn to page 83.

"Tonight we stay in the house of a friend. We must rest and get used to the thin air." Sangee leads the way to a group of houses made of stone. They are simple, lovely houses. On the small porches men, women, and children sit drinking tea. Chickens scratch at tufts of grass. High above, black birds with wingspans of nearly three meters soar on the rising air currents. At one end of the village are several thin poles with long, narrow prayer flags snaking in the light wind.

At all times you are aware of the immensity of the mountains. You have never been anywhere quite so silent, either.

Go on to the next page.

For three days you stay in this small village, taking short walks, testing your legs and lungs at this high altitude. On the afternoon of the third day, Sangee tells you that you are ready. "You are all strong. Your hearts have slowed down now. Your breathing is much better. We are ready to do the hard climbing at this altitude. We must hurry now. I have reports that the *Yeti* have been active in the Khumbu Icefall at Everest."

He pauses and looks first at you and then at Carlos. "It is long and hard and dangerous in the icefall. Great pieces of ice tumble from the glacier and pile up like children's building blocks. The ice may crack and give way when you least suspect. Many have died in these icefalls. You don't know which way to turn. Suddenly, great cracks open about you. Without warning, tons of ice come down upon you. Perhaps that is why the *Yeti* like the icefall. Few people will risk going there."

You understand the danger. It is well known that these regions have taken many lives. You had hoped that you could avoid the dangers of the Khumbu Icefall but such recent sightings of the *Yeti* are tempting. What should you do?

If you take the risks, turn to page 88.

If you can't decide, turn to page 89.

"I am ready, Runal. Lead the way."

Runal taps three times on the back of the buddha, near the spot where its skull and neck join. It makes a clanging sound like cymbals being struck.

Awesome! Before you stands a seven foot tall being, with broad shoulders and huge feet. His face is gentle and kind. You are not frightened.

Runal introduces him,"This is Zodak. He is your special guide. Follow him. He will take you where you must go."

"Can I say goodbye to Carlos?"

"It is not usual. I do not advise it; it might upset him and you. However, if you wish, go and say farewell."

If you do and bid farewell to Carlos,
turn to page 90.

If you decide against bidding farewell,
turn to page 92.

Secret worlds. This is all too scary.

To your way of thinking, you are not yet ready for this kind of thing. You want to explore the world you live in right now. Maybe Runal is crazy. Maybe he's a kidnapper. You'll never know.

You can walk out of the monastery, find Carlos, and continue the expedition.

That's what you came halfway around the world for, and that's what you intend to do. You collect Carlos from in front of the monastery and continue your search for the *Yeti*.

Months later you are no closer to success than you were at the start. The *Yeti* are elusive and your funds run out. You tried and tried hard. Your grandfather's words come back to you, "Everyone has the right to fail. Take chances; live life!"

The End

"Well, thank you for coming here. We thought it would be nice to study you, and it would have been hard for us to travel to your country." The *Yeti* laughs a low, long chuckle. The others grin. You look at Runal, at the helicopter pilot, at the surrounding mountains.

The *Yeti* continues, "Your friend is safe. He will be brought back to you later. Now we have had enough of you, and we hope you have had enough of us." The *Yeti* walk off and disappear into the icefall.

You find your way back to the smashed helicopter. Carlos is there, unharmed as they said. Your only disappointment is at not getting a picture.

It is several days before another helicopter finds you and makes a rescue. Tired, somewhat disappointed, you vow to continue your search for life forms in the remote regions of our planet.

The End

Four *Yeti* leap out from behind two huge seracs. You and Runal are captured immediately. The *Yeti*'s strength is unbelievable. Your arms are held in viselike grips. They carry you like sacks of rice, up further into the icefall. Finally, you are put down, and there in front of you is the helicopter pilot. He is unharmed. One of the *Yeti* speaks.

Turn to page 73.

You start down the trail, and right before your eyes a round orange-colored mass appears. It hovers near you. It's about the size of a beach ball.

ZAP! You are hit by a light beam. It feels as though you are being bathed in warm salt water. It's rather pleasant and removes all fear. You don't want to run or hide from this creature, whatever it is.

"Hey, it's cool. I'm not your enemy. I'm not bad. Who are you, or…or I mean, what are you?" You stand still, and several more of these round, glowing blobs gather round you.

"Earthling wishes knowledge. Earthling friendly. Release light beam. Sensor indicates Earthling is honest and speaks only truth."

The light beam switches off, and in a way you miss the comfort of its warmth. "I wish Carlos were here," you say.

Before your eyes Carlos appears! "Carlos! What's up? Where did you come from? This is weird."

Turn to page 78.

"Let's go back!"

Runal nods his agreement. This looks too much like a trap. You believe that Carlos left his pack as a warning to you.

Just as you slip out of the thicket, you see a huge creature, seven or more feet tall, weighing at least two hundred pounds, with short reddish fur covering its body. The creature has an oval, pointed head. Its feet are very wide and long. It sits next to the dead yak, eating.

You are nearly paralyzed with fear. But this may be your only chance to get a photograph!

If you take pictures, turn to page 91.

If you retreat into the thicket, turn to page 95.

78

Carlos smiles at you. "Hey, your wish was granted. That's the way it is with these Movidians. If they like you and believe in you, then your thoughts and wishes become real. I've been with them for the last two days. Up here in the mountains, things seem really clear and easy to understand. These mechanical creatures, well, they are higher beings. They use the mountains as their Earth base."

There is a humming sound, like cats purring. It's coming from the three creatures that Carlos calls Movidians.

One speaks again in a high, mechanical sounding voice.

"Time now for decision. We invite you to come with us to the Planet of the Seas in the Void of the Seven Moons. Will you come?"

If you go, turn to page 100.

If you refuse, explaining your mission to search for the Yeti, turn to page 102.

"Too wheeet, too wheeet, too tooooo."

You have trouble whistling, you are so nervous. Then you repeat the signal, only louder this time.

"Too wheeet, too wheeet, too tooooo."

There is a sudden crackling of bushes and twigs. You and Runal pull back ready to run for it. Carlos breaks out of the brush, sees you two, and yells, "Run for it, run for it!"

A camera dangles from his neck, and the three of you leap out of the thicket and make for the trail. You keep on going until you can go no further. Between gasps for breath, Carlos tells you that the *Yeti* carried him to the thicket and allowed him to photograph a group of sixteen *Yeti*. They told him that now he had what he needed and that they wanted to be left alone.

"Well, why were we invited?" you ask.

"To help me get back, I guess. I had no idea where I was."

You get back to the helicopter and return to Kathmandu with the first pictures the world has ever seen of the *Yeti*. Fame is now yours. It's the beginning of a great career.

The End

The door is too scary. Who knows what's behind it? The path, at least, is in the open. You scan the rock face, give one last look at the door, and edge off onto the path.

Within fifty paces you are up against a steep rock cliff. There seems to be no way out. Behind you the path disappears into a maze of trees. You hear the high-pitched call of the *Yeti*, loud and mocking.

A crackling sound makes you look up. A huge avalanche thunders down at more than 200 mph.

Turn to page 110.

82

With your heart thumping so hard you believe the whole world can hear it, you push the red door open. Inside is a tunnel with smooth walls illuminated by a gentle rose-colored light. There is no sign of life.

The tunnel winds on for several meters, and then ends abruptly. You find yourself standing in a long, narrow valley with steep walls leading to high, snow-covered peaks, probably Lhotse and Pumori from the look of them. The valley is warm, filled with flowering plants and trees, well guarded from strong winds.

A boy of eight or nine sits on a carved bench. He smiles at you and says in English, "Welcome. We thought you would come. Your friend Carlos is anxious to see you."

"Where is Carlos?"

"Oh, not far. If you wish to join him, you must agree never to go back to the world you came from. Do you understand?"

If you want to join Carlos, turn to page 98.

If you decide to leave, turn to page 96.

"You go ahead, Sangee. We'll stay here and keep watch."

He vanishes into the dark night. There is no wind, only the silence of mountains and sky and stars. Somewhere in the distance you hear the rumbling sound of water as it flows and drops from the glaciers that embrace Annapurna.

Carlos says, "We should go and help them. I feel selfish, sitting here safe and sound."

So near dawn you set off without your guide. The going is rough, and you no longer see the flashes of light. Above you towers Annapurna, with her white flanks of ice and snow. Then the sky lightens and the stars seem to disappear into the pale blue of the sky. Sunlight bursts on Machapuchhre. It seems to explode into gold and silver. Within minutes the light reaches Annapurna.

You stop for a cold breakfast of cheese and bread, washed down with tea.

Turn to page 99.

It takes you most of the night to thread your way down steep, tricky trails to reach the valley floor. Once there, you start up the immense Annapurna, scrambling over rocks and skirting the glacier. It is cold, and the night seems long to the three of you.

Several more times you see flickers of light. Now you are sure you have done the right thing. Someone needs help.

Near noon, Carlos says, "Stop. I think I see something."

Before your eyes, you see what you had come for. Dancing around a large fire are eleven *Yeti*. You have stumbled into a *Yeti* celebration at the end of the monsoons. You quietly watch, taking pictures and making notes. You have proved, at last, that the *Yeti* really exist.

Months later in Paris, France at the International Explorers Conference, you and Carlos are given their highest award for your work. Success is both exciting and lonely. Good luck.

The End

86

Click! The digital camera flashes with its solar battery-operated strobe.

What a creature! It's really a *Yeti!* It has a huge, hairy body, a giant head, enormous feet. It is frightened by the strobe, and it spots you. It heads right for you, making awful sounds—half growl, half gurgle.

If you run for it, turn to page 37.

If you stay put, and fire the camera strobe in hopes of scaring it off, turn to page 114.

You raise the ice axe. The *Yeti*, with eyes flashing, grabs it from your hands, snaps it as though it were a twig, and hurls it over the cliff.

The *Yeti* speaks in controlled tones.

"Leave us alone. Your world has enough. If we wanted what you have, your cities, your crimes, your wars, we would join you. But we don't want these things. Leave us alone. This is a warning."

With that, the *Yeti* leaves. You stand and look at the fleeting figure. What will you tell the International Foundation For Research Into Strange Phenomena?

The End

You go on into the icefall. The sun turns the Khumbu Icefall into a giant solar furnace. You squint, even though you're wearing your dark glacier goggles. Your down parkas are stuffed in the rucksacks, and you are in shirt sleeves. Sangee leads the way, cautiously skirting the huge, over-hanging blocks of ice, constantly probing the snow with his ice axe for a hidden crevasse—sure sign of a dangerous snow bridge.

You three are linked by a slender red-and-yellow rope that stretches between you.

Suddenly, with a whoop, three *Yeti* jump from their perch high above you and push a giant ice block. It quivers, and then it begins to tumble, slowly at first, then it picks up speed as it rolls toward you. Other seracs start to tumble around you, and you are locked forever in a sea of ice.

You didn't even have a chance to see the *Yeti*. All that remains is their eerie cry, echoing in the ice-filled valley.

The End

"Let's think about it, Sangee. The icefall is dangerous. The rains have weakened the ice and snow. Maybe it is a warning to us to leave this creature alone?"

Sangee nods his head. "As you wish, *bara sahib,* as you wish."

That night, all your supplies mysteriously disappear. It is further warning to leave things as they are in these high mountains. The *Yeti* have their own way of life, and they do not want you or anyone else to disturb it.

Regretfully you decide to withdraw and leave the *Yeti* to their lives in the high Himalayas. You know that it's the right thing to do.

The End

You walk out of the room. The *Yeti*, Zodak, accompanies you. Carlos stands outside, as he was when you left him. He is frozen in time. He can't hear you, nor can you hear him. You have become a part of a different world. You start to realize some of the consequences of your decision to go to Shangri-La.

You say a quiet goodbye to Carlos, even though he cannot hear you, and follow Zodak back into the monastery.

Turn to page 92.

Runal backs away from the creature. You advance very quietly and ease the lens cap from your digital camera.

Dropping to one knee you position the camera, framing the *Yeti* and its meal against a backdrop of Lhotse and Everest.

The digital camera records multiple images of the *Yeti*. The *Yeti* stops eating; his head arches up and around. He sniffs the air. Then he sees you.

Turn to page 101.

Zodak motions to you to follow. He takes one giant step into the air. You look with amazement as he hovers a meter off the ground. Then you step up into the air, and you, too, are suspended above the floor of the monastery. You are levitating.

Whoosh!! The two of you zoom out of the monastery, right through the walls, up into the sky. You travel at unimaginable speeds. You climb at a dizzying pace, until the two of you stand on top of the sharp, icy crest of Mt. Everest. Below you stretch glaciers, mountains, valleys. You see the world from the top.

Zodak points to a narrow slot near the topmost point of Mt. Everest. He says, "That is the route to Shangri-La." He takes three steps, enters the slot, and disappears from sight.

Turn to page 97.

"Back into the thicket! Hurry!"

You and Runal make a run for it. The *Yeti* is so busy eating that he pays no attention to the noises you two make.

"Now what? We can't go back that way, where the *Yeti* is, and we can't go deeper into this thicket where the others are."

As you finish speaking, the bushes in front of you are pushed aside. Three *Yeti* stand before you. The largest *Yeti* beckons you to follow. There is no choice but to do what he asks. The other two *Yeti* follow you and Runal. Any avenue of escape is cut off.

The pine and rhododendron bushes soon give way to a small clearing. At the far side is a smooth rock face perhaps a hundred meters high. On a group of boulders at the base of the rock sit a group of *Yeti*, varying in age and size. Carlos sits with them. He seems to be OK.

"Carlos! Hey, Carlos, what's happening?"

Carlos holds up his hand and says, "Listen to what they have to say."

Turn to page 106.

It's probably the best decision to leave. Don't look for trouble. But what about Carlos?

You wait for his return, and you wait and wait and wait and wait…

The End

You take one last look at the earth about you. You see the clouds rolling up from the flat, dry plains of the Punjab in India. You see the curve of the earth. You see the contrail of an airplane far to the south.

You step into the narrow chute. It's warm, glistening with the shine of a metal unknown to you. You hover in space in the narrow metal tube. In truth you are moving at a great speed down through the center of Everest. There is a rose-colored glow around you.

Where is Zodak? Some guide, you think, leaving you alone. What's next?

Turn to page 112.

98

You feel confident that once you get to Carlos the two of you can plan an escape. The child, who is dressed in a dark maroon robe similar to that worn by Buddhist monks, leads you down into the valley. As if by magic, the valley appears as a city of light. Its radiance astounds you. Its brilliance dazzles but does not blind. Your fear fades.

Turn to page 109.

Soon you are at a vertical wall of rock. Above it you see the face of the ice. Carlos drives the spike in; you both rope up and proceed slowly up the rock.

Over the rock, you meet an expanse of firm snow. But under it lies hard, cold ice. On with the crampons. You lead the way, probing carefully with your ice axe to seek out any hidden crevasse.

The climb seems endless, and even though you are only five thousand meters up, the air is thin and breathing is hard.

By mid-morning the sun is like a blast furnace. It reflects off the ice that surrounds you, and in the thin air the ultraviolet rays burn your skin. You both put white zinc ointment on your noses and lips.

You had taken a sight bearing when you saw the flashes, but that was at night. Now, in daylight, it is not easy to be sure just where the flashes came from. But you have a good sense of direction, so you keep going.

Near noon, you gain a crest, and then you see it. It's a Pilatus Courier aircraft, one used for mountain flying. It lies in the snow, crumpled like a forgotten toy. The tail section is twisted, but the wings are intact. The engine is buried in the snow.

Reaching the plane, you open the cabin door. Huddled in the plane are the pilot and two passengers. One of the passengers is unconscious. You do what you can for the people; later that day a Royal Nepal Airlines helicopter finds you. All is well. It was the right thing to give help in the mountains. Congratulations for a job well done.

The End

100

You and Carlos decide that it's too good an opportunity to pass up. You experience no fear or real hesitation. Maybe that has something to do with the light beam that seemed to wash away fear and doubt.

The head Movidian hovers near you. You even imagine that it is smiling, in spite of the fact that it has no face.

"What do we call you?" you ask. For a moment, there is just the humming of electrical circuits.

Then the Movidian answers, "You may call me Norcoon. I am an X52 Double A, intelligent, mobile activator being. I am head of this advance party. We will call you Earth One and Earth Two."

With a hiss, the creatures sink to the ground, where they sit and glow. Norcoon says, "Please, it is easier to travel to the Planet of the Seas in the Void of the Seven Moons if you remove your body and let your mind float free."

You look over at Carlos. What does this creature mean by "remove your body"?

"How? I mean, we are our bodies," says Carlos.

Norcoon points his light beam at you, and once again you feel the warmth and pleasure you felt before. Fear vanishes and, before you know it, you are free.

Turn to page 104.

You freeze. The camera slips out of your hands.

The *Yeti* jumps up with a roar and lunges at you. Before you know what has happened, the *Yeti* has you in its grasp.

Runal leaps forward, swinging the ice axe that he carries as a walking stick. He hits the *Yeti* three times on the shoulders with the flat face of the axe. The blows are as effective as a mosquito bite.

From out of nowhere comes a sharp whistle-like call, and the *Yeti* suddenly drops you to the ground. You are shocked and unable to move.

The woman from the house appears.

Turn to page 103.

"No, we can't go. We must finish our expedition." You feel fear begin to creep back. You don't trust this thing.

Suddenly three Movidians turn on their light beams. Wham! Carlos is hit with the beam, and he vanishes.

The head Movidian says, "Earth creature, don't be foolish. Join us. You will never regret it."

You start moving toward the side of the trail. No fast moves, just slow steps that don't seem to bother these strange creatures. You keep talking the entire time.

"Tell me more. I mean, what's it like up on the Planet of the Seas?"

"Oh, it is beautiful. You will like it. It is one of the higher realms. Only successful Earth creatures ever get to go there."

You ask, "What do you mean successful Earth creatures? What makes Carlos and me so successful?"

The Movidian glows a brighter color orange. You reach down, picking up a fist-sized rock, and, in a sweeping move, hurl it at the glowing blob. Just at that point several *Yeti* come running. They are swinging great clubs. They slash rapidly in the air next to the Movidians, dodging the light beams. With a frantic gurgle, followed by a high-speed whoosh, the blobs depart.

Carlos reappears and, knowing the *Yeti* are now your allies, the two of you start to learn to communicate with them.

The End

The woman speaks rapidly in a tongue neither you nor Runal can understand. It's more a series of low grunts, mixed with high piercing whistles. The Yeti seems to become quiet, almost docile. The Yeti and the woman disappear into the thicket, leaving the two of you stunned and confused but safe to return to Kathmandu with your pictures.

Years later you entertain your grandchildren with stories of finding the Yeti.

The End

Pure mind—no matter.

Norcoon approves, and offers you space aboard his mechanical transporter. Inside the pumpkin shape there is plenty of room for you and Carlos and all your thoughts.

"Now, my friends, we are on our way to the Planet of the Seas. It's where all thoughts end up."

You whirl away, confident that one day you will return wiser and better able to help others in a world where the going is rough.

The End

106

You and Runal are made to sit in front of the group of *Yeti*. Your guards stand uneasily behind you. A *Yeti* of medium height, with a grayish tinge to his fur, stands and looks at you.

"You wanted to find us. Well, now you have. If you wish, take pictures. If you wish, record our voices. But listen well, listen and learn so that all will benefit."

His voice has a firm yet relaxed quality that erases your fear. Runal is actually smiling. Suddenly, it occurs to you that maybe he knew what was going on all the time.

The *Yeti* walks slowly around the circle of beings. He stops, looks to the sky and the mountains, and speaks.

Turn to page 111.

One last chance, is that it? Is that what you want? OK. You're on. Out of the valley of Shangri-La and back to the real world. Is it different? Can you do whatever you want? Can you fulfill your dreams? Can you enjoy your life completely? Or must you be content within limits?

The End

With gliding motions, you fly along a pathway. It feels as though you have been there before.

"We are here. Please enter." The boy points the way to a building that shimmers with light. It reminds you of the Taj Mahal, except it has many more towers, and the main dome is surrounded by hundreds of smaller domes, almost like leaves of a flower.

You take several steps forward, and then feel the grasping of a force not unlike magnetic force. You are held in the force field for several seconds, and then transported to the innermost room of the building.

Turn to page 60.

110

You huddle against the rock wall. The avalanche thunders by. Miraculously, you escape unharmed, except for choking on the snow crystals in the air.

Maybe you should get out now and go back to the red door.

Turn to page 82.

"In the beginning of time on this planet, life was difficult but simple. Survival was what held us together. We took the lives of only those things we needed to feed us. Nothing more."

A slight wind moves the branches of the pines. The *Yeti* continues his tale.

"Later, people found fire, lived in villages, later small towns, then bigger and bigger cities. They made weapons to hunt and then to protect themselves from animals and others Then they began to make war on each other. We, the *Yeti*, retreated, wanting none of the war nor the towns. We kept on retreating until there was no place left to go. So here we are, high in the mountains, where we thought we were safe."

"But you are safe. We mean no harm."

"Perhaps not you, but there are others who do. Leave us alone. Return to your own lands. If you want cities and war and this thing they call pollution, then live with them or get rid of them. But leave us be."

The group of *Yeti* nods in agreement. The meeting is over, and you, Carlos, and Runal are allowed to leave. You decide not to take pictures or record their voices. You also decide to suggest to the International Foundation For Research Into Strange Phenomena that a better study would be of the so-called civilized world.

The End

With a gentle bump, you come to rest. In front of you is a clear glass door. You push it open. There stands Zodak.

"Come. Welcome to Shangri-La."

You walk out into a dark green valley surrounded by low-lying hills. In the distance are high mountains. One of them looks like Everest. You hear music unlike any music you have ever heard before. It is somewhat like the sounds in the monastery, the bells and wind. The sunlight is warm and relaxing.

Go on to the next page.

Zodak leads you down a long trail to a seven-story building. It seems to be a fortress, but it is painted white and red and gold. There are no soldiers, no guns, only people who smile and greet you as though you are an old friend.

It seems so natural. You turn to Zodak, and you get a shock. His form has changed. Now he is the mirror image of you! What does this mean?

Although you never find out about that, you learn about many things as you stay in the valley. You have the chance to try many activities you could never try before—but only what is available in the valley. You learn to be contented within the limits of the small valley.

Second thoughts?

Turn to page 107.

114

The digital camera keeps on flashing its strobe. The *Yeti* stops in its tracks, searches frantically for something, a friend perhaps, and then turns and, with amazing speed, vanishes into the night.

Unfortunately for you, the shutter in your digital camera mysteriously jams.

The End

116

You look at Runal, you look at the monastery, and you look at Carlos.

"No, I'm not ready to accept your offer."

No sooner have you spoken the words than clouds choke the narrow valley. The mountains seem to vanish, and the monastery is swallowed up by darkness. Runal turns his back to you and speaks as if to the wind.

"I am very sorry that you cannot accept. Since you do not feel that you can go ahead, the expedition is declared over. All permits are revoked. You must return to Kathmandu and leave the country in twenty-four hours."

The note of finality in Runal's voice tells you that you have no choice whatsoever. Your trip is over.

The End

GLOSSARY

Base camp – A designated location on the lower part of the mountain where a climbing expedition sets up tents and leaves supplies and personnel. Once base camp is functional, climbers move on to their final destination carrying backpacks of only essential supplies and equipment. Base camp serves as the communications hub of the climb. On their descent, climbers often arrive at base camp in need of rest, medical attention, and food.

Carpe diem – A Latin term meaning "seize the day". The phrase encourages people to enjoy the pleasures of today instead of worrying about the future.

Glacier – A huge mass of very slow moving ice that is made from compacted snow and flows over a mountain or other land mass.

Himalayas – A 1,500 mile mountain range in south-central Asia that is home to nine of the ten tallest peaks in the world. Mount Everest, the tallest mountain in the world, is part of the Himalayan Mountain range. The range goes through the countries of Kashmir, northern India, Tibet, Nepal, Sikkim and Bhutan.

Ice axe – An axe used by climbers to cut holes in the ice for their hands and feet in order to climb higher. When faced with a sheer wall of ice, cutting footholds and handholds allows climbers to scale the ice.

Incense – Material that is burned and produces a pleasant, almost spicy, smell. The burning of incense is part of some religious ceremonies.

Meter – A unit of measurement that is equal to 39.37 inches. The metric system, a measurement system based on meters, is now the international standard for measurement.

Mountaineer – A person who climbs mountains as a sport. Mountaineers enjoy the challenge of climbing various peaks despite the many dangers involved.

Poacher – A person who kills or captures wild animals illegally. Poachers are usually trespassing (going to places where they are not allowed). As with other criminals, poachers will use violence and desperate means to avoid being caught by the police or local authorities.

Serac – A sharp needle of ice found in the crevasses or "cracks" of a glacier.

Shangri-la – An imaginary place that is very beautiful and where life is perfect. Many stories have been written about Shangri-la, but since it is not real, descriptions of it vary.

Yak – A type of ox that has long, shaggy hair and lives in the mountains of central Asia and Tibet. Yaks can be wild or domesticated, meaning kept by humans as animals would be on a farm.

Yeti – A name for the "Abominable Snowman". "Yeti" in Tibetan means "magical creature". Legend has it that the Abominable Snowman, a large, hairy human-like creature, lives in the Himalayan Mountains. Sightings of the Abominable Snowman are cloaked in mystery and typically unreliable. There is no proof that this mystical creature actually exists, although there is one photo of a Yeti taken in 1954.

CREDITS

This book is the work of many people. R. A. Montgomery reviewed and edited the original manuscript, bringing it into the Internet age. Shannon Gilligan, along with Laura Arnesen at Chooseco LLC and Judy Cooper, Kate McQuade, Marlene Stemple, and Ellen Maxwell at Sundance Publishing, nursed it through various stages of editorial and artistic development. Stacey Hood at Big Eyedea Visual Design in Waitsfield, Vermont, was responsible for layout and design, with help from Bonnie Atwater. We are indebted to Dave Zahn at Signal Advertising for his guidance on fonts. Sally Reisner proofread and corrected the final words. Caitlin LaBarge provided invaluable final input as our 'cold reader'. Laura Sanderson kept everyone informed and on track. Gordon Troy performed the legal pirouettes that result in proper trademark and copyright protections. Last but not least, Sherry Litwack and Bob Laronga at Sundance acted as godparents. *A very special thanks to Wick Van Heuven.*

Illustrator: Laurence Peguy was born and raised in les Landes, one of the most beautiful regions of France. She received her Baccalaureate in 1997 in Literature, attended the Visual Art Institute of Orleans, and graduated from The Emile Cohl School of Animation in 2002. She has worked as a cartoon portraitist at Epcot Center at Disneyworld, Florida. She currently works for the French creative group "2 Minutes" as a Flash animator. This is her first *Choose Your Own Adventure®* book.

Cover Artist: Jose Luis Marron lives and works in Madrid. He has studied film at universities in Canada and France. Jose worked for several years in the Spanish film and television industry, before turning to design and illustration full-time. He has illustrated seven *Choose Your Own Adventure®* covers.

ABOUT THE AUTHOR

R. A. MONTGOMERY has hiked in the Himalayas, climbed mountains in Europe, scuba-dived in Central America, and worked in Africa. He lives in France in the winter, travels frequently to Asia, and calls Vermont home. Montgomery graduated from Williams College and attended graduate school at Yale University and NYU. His interests include macro-economics, geo-politics, mythology, history, mystery novels, and music. He has two grown sons, a daughter-in-law, and two granddaughters. His wife, Shannon Gilligan, is an author and noted interactive game designer. Montgomery feels that the new generation of people under 15 is the most important asset in our world.

Visit us online at CYOA.com for games and other fun stuff, or to write to R. A. Montgomery!